Follow
the
Money!

written and illustrated by
Loreen Leedy

Holiday House New York

for Mary Cash

Copyright © 2002 by Loreen Leedy
All Rights Reserved
Printed in the United States of America
www.holidayhouse.com
First Edition

Library of Congress Cataloging-in-Publication Data
Leedy, Loreen.
Follow the money! / written and illustrated by Loreen Leedy.
p.   cm.
Summary: A quarter describes all the ways
it is used from the time it is minted
until it is taken back to a bank.
ISBN 0-8234-1587-2 (hardcover)
1. Money—Juvenile literature. 2. Coins—Juvenile literature.
3. Coins—United States—Juvenile literature.
[1. Money—United States—Juvenile literature.] I. Title.
HG221.5.L433 2002
—dc21   2001039418

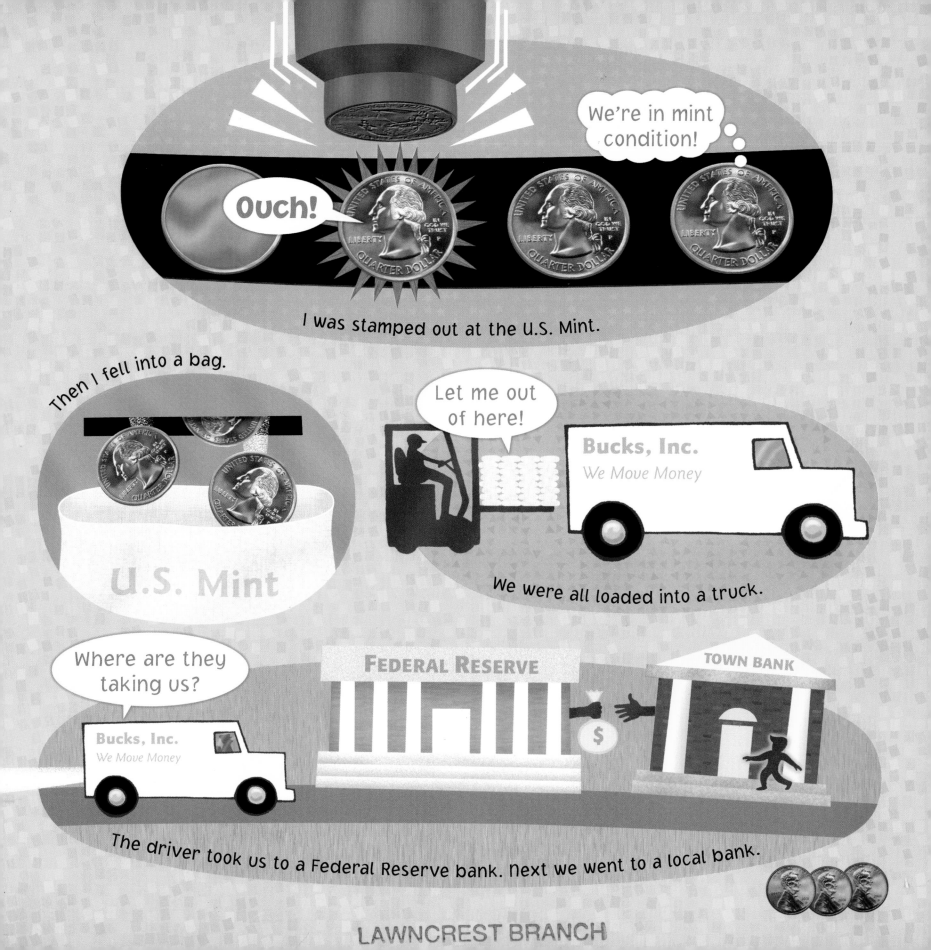

We finally slowed down.

The lady gave me to the clown in exchange for a balloon.

The boy took us on a ride.

He used us to buy a toy airplane.

That'll be fifteen dollars.

$15

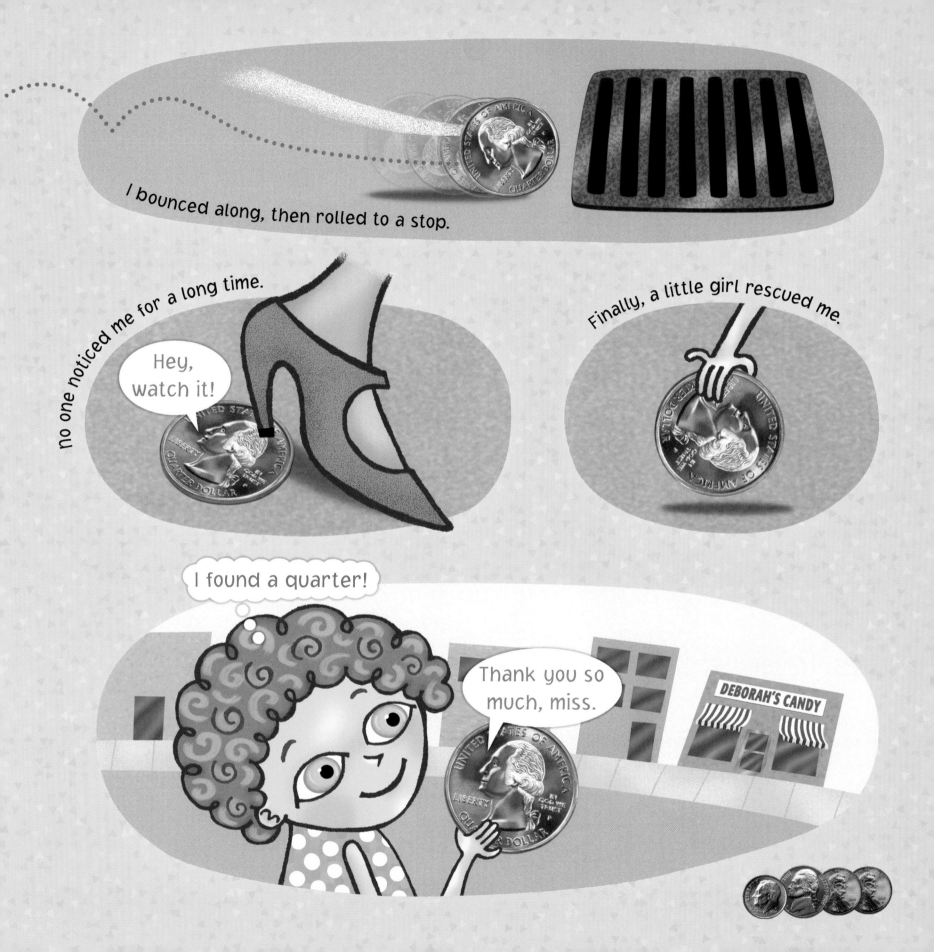

After a long time, Bob's wife took out the laundry.

I was back in the bank again.

More About Money

Who Needs Money?

Before there was money, there was barter. People traded goods or services directly.

One problem with bartering is that you may not have what the other person wants.

It can be difficult to carry and store the items you have to trade.

It is hard to save up for the future without money.

People all over the world looked for something durable and easily carried to use for money. In the past, a variety of objects were used, including beads, stones, and salt. Metals such as copper, gold, and silver became popular and are still used today to make coins. These days, most money is in the form of paper bills.

beads

stones

salt

shells

feathers

Money in the United States

The currency in the U.S.A. has had many different designs. The paper bills have recently been redesigned (including the five-dollar bill and larger). One reason is to make it more difficult for criminals to print counterfeit money. Check for these features to make sure a bill is authentic.

Security Thread
Hold the bill up to a light to see the words "USA TWENTY" and a tiny flag. Each denomination's security thread is in a different position.

Watermark
Hold the bill up to a light to see a hidden portrait (similar to the main portrait).

Color-shifting ink
The number in the lower right corner looks green when viewed directly; it's black when viewed at an angle. (All of the redesigned bills except the five-dollar bill have this ink).

Microprinting
Each bill has very small printing that is readable with a magnifier.

Paper
The paper feels sturdy and has red and blue fibers in it.

Fine-line Printing Patterns
The fine lines behind the portrait are difficult to copy.

To find out more about paper money, visit the Web site of the Bureau of Engraving at **www.bep.treas.gov.**

Coins are made by the U.S. Mint in one of four locations: Philadelphia, PA; Denver, CO; San Francisco, CA; West Point, NY. Tours are available.

In 1998, the U.S. Mint began the 50 States Quarters™ program, which has been very popular. A custom-designed quarter for each state will be issued one by one until all fifty states are released by 2008. Many people, young and old, have enjoyed collecting the special quarters. For more information about the program and U.S. coins in general, visit the Mint's Web site at **www.usmint.gov.**

Money Words

allowance	an amount of money given regularly, such as once a week
bank	a business that stores and lends money
bargain	something sold at a low price
barter	to trade goods or services directly without using money
cash	money in the form of coins or bills
cent	one penny; one hundredth of a dollar
change	coins
charity	an organization that helps a cause, such as homeless animals
counterfeit	worthless copy
currency	money
dime	ten cents; one tenth of a dollar
dollar	a coin or bill worth one hundred pennies
donate	to give money, goods, or services to a charity
earn	to get money by working for it
half-dollar	fifty cents; one half of a dollar
loan	money paid to someone that must be paid back
mint	to produce coins by stamping metal; the place authorized by the government to manufacture coins
nickel	five cents; one twentieth of a dollar
owe	to be obligated to pay back a loan
payday	the day workers get paid
penny	one cent; one hundredth of a dollar
penny-pincher	a person who spends very little money
quarter	twenty-five cents; one quarter of a dollar
save	to keep money for a particular purpose
wage	payment to a worker